New Girl
in School

Activity Book

T0355241

Name _____

Age _____

Class _____

OXFORD
UNIVERSITY PRESS

OXFORD

UNIVERSITY PRESS

Great Clarendon Street, Oxford OX2 6DP

Oxford University Press is a department of the University of Oxford.
It furthers the University's objective of excellence in research, scholarship,
and education by publishing worldwide in

Oxford New York

Auckland Bangkok Buenos Aires Cape Town Chennai
Dar es Salaam Delhi Hong Kong Istanbul Karachi Kolkata
Kuala Lumpur Madrid Melbourne Mexico City Mumbai
Nairobi São Paulo Shanghai Taipei Tokyo Toronto

OXFORD and OXFORD ENGLISH are registered trade marks of
Oxford University Press in the UK and in certain other countries

ISBN: 978 0 19 440162 3

Printed in China

Activities by: Christine Lindop
Illustrations by: Annabel Tempest
Original story by: Christine Lindop

Connect.

cut

fold

paste

skip

sweep

swim

switch off

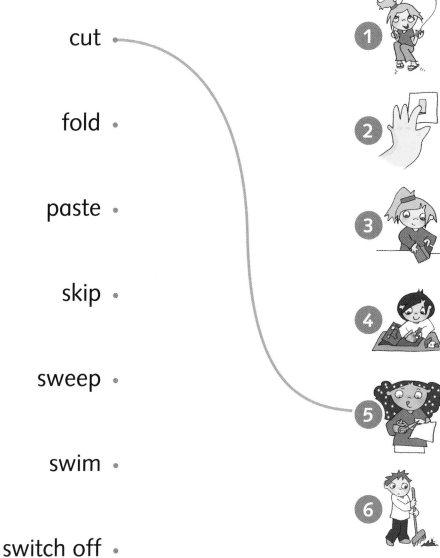

Connect.

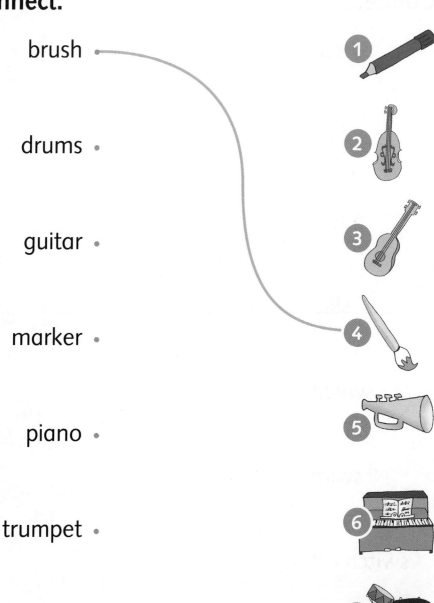

brush

drums

guitar

marker

piano

trumpet

violin

1 **Circle the odd one out.**

❶ orange (student) banana apple

❷ shoe hat jeans office

❸ dog cat moon frog

❹ take desk sofa chair

❺ blue yellow black like

❻ noses looks eyes ears

2 **Complete using the circled words.**

Linda is a new ___student___. She is in the

_____ with Miss Taylor. There is a

_____ on Linda's bag. "Please

_____ Linda to Class 4C," says

Miss Taylor. "I _____ your bag,

Linda," says Emma. The cat _____

at Linda.

Circle the correct words.

❶ Linda, Peter, and Emma are
   ~~painting~~ cutting folding .

❷ Emma is painting a dog cat horse .

❸ There are clouds moons stars
   in Linda's hair.

❹ The cat is near the table brush
   window .

❺ There are six pictures of trees trains
   trucks .

❻ Emma's eyes are blue green brown .

❼ Emma looks at the
   birds brushes board .

❽ Then she looks at the
   paint pen paper .

❾ There are three five
   eight brushes.

Circle yes or no .

❶ The children are in the yard.　　(yes)　no

❷ Peter is skipping.　　yes　no

❸ Linda is flying.　　yes　no

❹ Peter and Emma can't fly.　　yes　no

❺ The children are
looking at Emma.　　yes　no

❻ The cat is looking
at the birds.　　yes　no

❼ One girl is pointing at Linda.　　yes　no

❽ There are six birds
in the tree.　　yes　no

❾ There are four boys
in the yard.　　yes　no

1 **Complete the puzzle.**

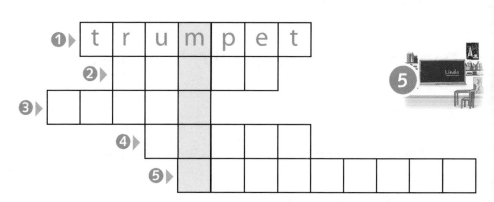

What is the secret word? _____

2 **Answer the questions.**

Can you play the piano? _____

Can you play the guitar? _____

Can you play the drums? _____

Circle yes or no .

❶ The cat is eating pizza.   yes   (no)

❷ The children are in
the lunchroom.   yes   no

❸ There is a cookie
near Emma's head.   yes   no

❹ Peter is sitting next to Linda.   yes   no

❺ There is a clock on the table.   yes   no

❻ The children are looking
at the cookies.   yes   no

❼ Linda is very hungry.   yes   no

❽ There is a drink in
Peter's hand.   yes   no

❾ Linda makes six cookies.   yes   no

Answer the questions.

❶ How many frogs are there? _____ five _____

❷ How many ducks are there? _____

❸ How many brown birds are there?

_____

❹ How many cats are there? _____

❺ How many teachers are there?

_____

❻ How many brushes are there? _____

❼ How many children are there? _____

❽ How many bags are there? _____

❾ How many butterflies are there?

_____

❿ How many red stars are there?

_____

Connect.

❶ The children are

❷ They are helping •

❸ Emma puts •

❹ Linda puts •

❺ Mrs. Young says •

❻ The cat is •

❼ There is a green book •

❽ There are five books •

❾ Peter is collecting •

❿ Two girls are •

• the books.

• thank you.

• in the library.

• under Peter's arm.

• the chairs back.

• near the door.

• on a chair.

• in Linda's arms.

• the teacher.

• the books away.

Complete the sentences.

> in   wrong   mom   Class 4C   must
> desk   skirt   brushes   office   stars

❶ Miss Taylor goes to __Class 4C__ .

❷ Linda is not at her _____ .

❸ Linda is in the _____ .

❹ Linda's bag is _____ her hand.

❺ The _____ are in Linda's bag.

❻ Linda's _____ is in the office too.

❼ She has a beautiful purple _____ .

❽ There are _____ in her eyes.

❾ Linda is at the _____ school.

❿ She _____ go to the Magic School.

Circle yes or no .

❶ Linda and her mother
are flying.   (yes)   no

❷ They are saying hello.   yes   no

❸ They are going to
the Magic School.   yes   no

❹ The cat is sleeping.   yes   no

❺ The children are
playing basketball.   yes   no

❻ The children are
saying goodbye.   yes   no

❼ Mrs. Young is in the office.   yes   no

❽ Miss Taylor is in the yard.   yes   no

❾ The children had
a good time.   yes   no

Answer the questions.

❶ Where does Emma take Linda?
She takes her to Class 4C.

❷ How does Linda paint flowers?

❸ What does Linda do in the yard?

❹ What does Peter play?

❺ What can you see on Linda's desk?

❻ Who puts the books away?

❼ Where must Linda go?

❽ How does she go there?

Complete the crossword.

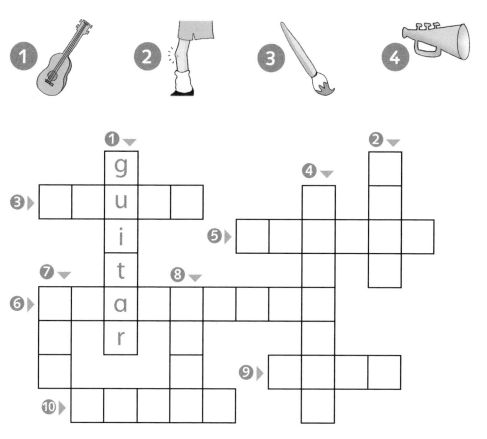

Complete the story.

Linda was the new girl in

_____school_____. Emma took

her to _____. In the yard,

Linda said, "_____ with me."

Then she _____ the piano,

the _____, and the drums. Mrs.

Young looked at Linda's _____.

There were five _____ and

_____ ducks there! The children

played _____. Then they

_____ the teacher in the library.

Linda went to the _____.

Her _____ was there. Linda was

at the _____ school. She said

_____ to her friends and went to

the Magic _____ with her mom.